GOD IS UP TO SOMETHING CONCERNING YOU!

BY
NANCY F. LOWERY

God is Up to Something Concerning YOU!
Copyright © 2018 by Nancy Lowery

ISBN: 978-1732529304

Unless otherwise noted, all Scripture quotations are taken from the New King James Version of the Bible. All scriptures that contain words in bold print are made by the author for emphasis and meaning and are not found in the original biblical text. All parentheticals within the scripture quotation are commentary by the author and not found in the original scripture.

All rights reserved. No part of this book may be reproduced, stored in a retrieval system, or transmitted in any form or by any means - electronic, mechanical, photocopy, recording, or any other, without permission in writing from the author.

Printed in the United States of America

ENDORSEMENTS

From the moment I met her, I recognized that I was in the presence of an extraordinary person. There was a radiance about her that revealed inner strength that is understandable only if the person is acquainted with God. That first impression has only deepened with time.

Nancy Lowery is on speaking terms with God. When Nancy prays, you can tell that she is one who practices the art of praying without ceasing. Her life and witness is a prayer. She is quick to say, "I will pray for you." You know instinctively that this is true. You are grateful that she is on your side and that she talks with the God who is on your side too.

The term that best describes Nancy is "Care Giver." She has many gifts of the Holy Spirit for ministry. She is further gifted by unusual care for people. She gives care freely. I have witnessed her constancy in caring for the sick. Hers is a caring that goes beyond mere sentiment and is a healing force. It is filled with love. She loves the Lord and she loves people. It shows.

Nancy is steeped in the scriptures. She draws on the Bible constantly. She is wise. She is educated. She is articulate. She is true, and she is a splendid servant of

God. This explains why this book is a treasure. I am honored to commend her and this book to you!

Dr. Harold K. Bales

*****

Nancy Lowery is a person who I consider to be a wonderful friend as well as a spiritual leader. She is always willing to help out in situations where care and time are involved. Her smile and easy manner makes her very approachable. She is often available at a moment's notice to give a helping hand, to say a prayer with or for you, and to answer a question.

Nancy is invaluable. She knows the meaning of prayer and hope. Oftentimes she will join forces with a person or family facing a difficult situation. Talking and praying with them comes easily to Nancy.

In conclusion, it is easy to talk about a person who has many outstanding qualities like kindness, empathy and intelligence. Nancy is an individual who is admired by many.

Your Friend and Big Sis,
Mrs. E. Flowers

SPECIAL TRIBUTES

I am who I am today because of my Heavenly Father and three *phenomenal* women.

First and foremost, I want to acknowledge the matriarch of our family, my great grandmother, Mrs. Nancy Smith Tolbert. (I am elated to be her namesake). She was a hard-working woman who possessed quiet strength and could light up a room with her beautiful smile.

My great grandmother never met a stranger, and would graciously feed anyone who entered her home, regardless of race. I can recall sitting on her lap as a little child, while she softly sang, "You are my Sunshine". For years I thought she created that song just for ME! She left a proud and powerful legacy for her descendants to cherish and emulate.

Secondly, I am truly grateful for my grandmother, Mrs. Ruby Leach, whom I affectionately called "Mama Ruby". Her love and support of me was unwavering.
She had so much *resiliency*. My grandmother did **not** mince her words. She said what she meant and meant what she said! I learned my culinary skills from her at a very early age. YES, my grandmother spoiled me and

called me her "Princess". She always made me feel so very special.

Last but certainly not least, I want to honor the woman who birthed me, my beautiful soft-spoken and very intelligent mother, Mrs. Mary R. Foster. I love and miss her with every fiber of my being! She was my ROCK, my mentor, and my "she-ro".

My mother's love for me knew no boundaries. She led by example and took me to church, where I could learn more about the unconditional love of God. She stressed the importance of putting Him first, in all that I do, and to do all things in excellence. Rest in Heaven my beloved Mother!

DEDICATION

This book is lovingly dedicated to the memories of the following people in my life:

My precious and beloved Mother-in-Love, Mrs. Janie Mae Lowery (she was my Naomi and I was her Ruth). I miss her so much! My loving and compassionate Father-in-law, Rev. Willie Nash, Jr. My brother-in-law James "Pee Wee" Lowery, who I never had the opportunity to meet, and my very special uncle, Mr. Paul Tolbert.

Several of my special and loveable Aunts, who left their indelible impressions in my heart: Mrs. Carrie B. Thompson, Mrs. Pauline T. Forney, Mother Fannie Leach, Mrs. Goldie Johnson, Mrs. Clezell Black, Pastor Willie Scott and Mrs. Ernestine Staton. They were such positive people and always had nuggets of wisdom and inspiring words to share.

My very special friends and confidants: Minister Virginia Williamson Bost, Rev. Doris H. Crudup, Mrs. Katie Mae Vereen, Mrs. Jennie Gray and Elder Bessie Mae Griffith.

I will forever be grateful for the prayers and loving kindness you ALL have showered upon my life!

ACKNOWLEDGEMENTS

I give **all** the Glory, Honor and Highest Praise to the Father, the Son and the Holy Spirit, for choosing and using me as a willing vessel to write this book.

I also want to honor my husband Malcom Angelo Lowery (my Honey-Bunny) for being so patient with me as I sacrificed endless hours working on this book. He has been my confidant, friend, lover and greatest supporter, in all that the Lord has called me to do. I love him "just because".

I am also grateful for the love and support of our daughter, Professor Shana Lowery, and my inner circle of family, extended family, clergy and friends.

As a veteran myself, I would like to pay special homage to **all** military personnel, including active duty, reserved, retired, disabled, POW's, MIA's, veterans and those who lost their lives in the patriotic line of duty, and their families. We are constantly reminded that Freedom isn't Free. Thank you all for serving and defending the United States of America.

I would also like to acknowledge **all** educators, health care workers, survivors of cancer, domestic abuse and catastrophic disasters!

There are some Gospel Music Artists who have ministered to my spirit and soul during times of gladness and sadness. These singers are very dear to my heart, and they include: Bishops Marvin Sapp, Paul Morton, Rance Allen and William Murphy. Pastors John P. Kee, Shirley Caesar, Nancy Harmon and Donnie McClurkin. I would be remiss if I failed to recognize the Winans, Donald Lawrence, Yolanda Adams, Dottie Peebles, The William Brothers, The Gaithers, The Mighty Clouds of Joy, Tamela Mann, Vicki Yohe and Dr. Bobby Jones. Thank you **all** for sharing your gifts and allowing the anointing upon your lives to bless me and millions of others!

Lastly, I want to send a special shout-out to Lonnie Hunter, a former DJ on Praise 100.9. He had a segment on his show called, "GET IT DONE" Thursday. God really used him to motivate, irritate, challenge and inspire me and countless others to stop procrastinating and **GET IT DONE!** Whether your **"it"** was starting a business, getting your degree, producing a play or writing a BOOK.

Because of **prayers and persistence,** I FINALLY wrote my first book entitled, "Are YOU a Chosen Vessel?"

To God be the Glory, I have now completed my SECOND book!

TABLE OF CONTENTS

God's Purpose for Your Life……………....………1

The Promises of God…………………………...........6

My Condition is Not My Conclusion…..…...............10
The Woman with the Issue of Blood, J.R. Martinez

It's Not Over Until God Says It's Over………...........18
Mr. and Mrs. Job, How Hannah got her Joy Back

God is Able to Turn it Around…………...…………36

A Notice to Satan…………………………………...39

What I Start With, is Not What I'm Stuck With……42
Steve Harvey

Wise Sayings………………………………………47

I Don't Look Like What I've Been Through………50
Tamar (Not Tamar Braxton), Three Hebrew Boys

The Favor of God…………………………..............63
Nehemiah, Esther and Jabez

God Can Still Bless a Hot Mess……………………...71
The Prodigal Son, The Woman at the Well

God is Up to Something Concerning YOU!……….84
My Real Testimony

About the Author……………………………….....95

1
GOD'S PURPOSE FOR YOUR LIFE

You may think that you have already laid out the plans for your own life, have the formula for your success and have your life all figured out. I hate to burst your bubble, but have you ever heard the expression: *If you want to make God laugh, just tell Him **your** plans*? If you are a child of God, your purpose has already been **assigned and designed by GOD.**

Jeremiah 29:11 states: "For I know the plans that I have for you declares the Lord, plans to prosper you and not harm you, plans to give you hope and a future".

God's plan is so much better, brighter and greater than anything you could ever imagine for yourself!

Have you ever questioned God by asking, "Who am I?" "What have I been put on earth to do?" "What is my **purpose**?" Has God ever responded to your question?

According to Romans 8:28, it is clear: "And we know that ALL things work together for good to them that love God, to them who are the called according to **His purpose**".

God will fulfill every purpose He has for you. He will work ALL things, including your life, according to His Master Plan. God planned your life long before you were ever born, and your assistance was not required. He has a specific purpose and plan for each individual. God chooses and uses **everything** we go through in life, to prepare us for our DESTINY. His thoughts and His ways are not our thoughts and ways. They are so much higher than ours!

Your purpose includes your personality, imperfections, gifts, talents, abilities and most of all your DESTINY. Let me set the record straight by saying, "Your **problems** do NOT dictate your **purpose**".

We have all encountered hurts, disappointments, setbacks, obstacles, criticisms and rejections. Many of us know what it feels like to become faint-hearted, grow weary, and want to give up and throw in the towel, because of so much pain, pressure and unmet expectations. Even while reading this chapter, you may feel like you're at the end of your **rope**, but it doesn't mean you have to be at the end of your **hope!**

Romans 8:24-25 (NIV) states: "We are saved by hope. But hope that is seen is no hope at all. Who hopes for what they already have? But if we hope for what we do not yet have, then we patiently wait for it".

Our DESTINY is determined by our DECISIONS. To prepare for your DESTINY, you must be willing to do **whatever** God requires for you to do **NOW,** in order to be ready for your **NEXT**. By your next I mean your next opportunity, challenge, level, and even your next season (which is your destiny).

It's time for God's chosen people to believe that in spite of your past, God is behind the scenes changing, rearranging, and preparing you to walk into your **NEXT.** You must believe down in your spirit, that you are next in line for a miracle, a promotion, increase, elevation, a breakthrough, to receive the blessings and favor of an Almighty God!

Yes, I know that you think you're waiting on God to do the supernatural; but before that happens, you must first do the natural! You must stir up the gifts God has already placed within you. You must walk by FAITH, and not by SIGHT. You must call those things that be not, as though they were. You must press past your obstacles!

It takes "crazy faith" to believe that God wants to intentionally choose, use and bless you, *in spite of* you! Our Heavenly Father wants you to believe that no one else on earth, can tell you what you're worth! It doesn't matter if so-called friends have deleted you from Facebook or excluded you from their superficial cliques. You have to be confident in knowing if God is **for you**, and it doesn't even matter who may be against you!

Beloved, you are not defined by your past or the size of your bank account. You are about more than the size of your hips, lips and your fingertips.

The devil doesn't want you to know this, but YOU matter to God. Who you are matters, what you feel matters, and what you've gone through matters to God. When Satan tries to bring up your past, you need to tell him what the Bible says in 1 Corinthians 15:10a: "By the **Grace of God, I am who I am**". You my dear are who **GOD** says you are, regardless of whom you're around!

Lastly, let me be real with you! Many times, while we're waiting to fulfill our purpose, we will endure some pain in the process. But thanks be unto God, **His strength** is made perfect in our weakness. And ALL of our trials and tests are just opportunities for God to show up and demonstrate His power and presence in our lives! You are a person of purpose, with great potential. You are capable of doing amazing things!

God has a strategic purpose and plan for your life. You may not understand it, but I double dare you to TRUST HIM! Proverbs 3:5-6 sums this chapter up by saying: "Trust in the Lord with all your heart and lean not to your own understanding. In all your ways acknowledge Him, and He **shall** direct your paths".

If people forget my name, or if no songs, books or poems are ever written about me, that's perfectly okay, because I want to fulfill God's divine purpose and plan for my life. By faith, I declare and decree that I am DESTINED for GREATNESS!

What is YOUR Confession of Faith?

2
THE PROMISES OF GOD

Webster defines the word PROMISE as "a pledge, oath, vow or an agreement to do or not to do something". Usually we have the best of intentions when we make a promise. Sometimes we make promises to ourselves, and after a certain amount of time has passed, we tend to "renege" (it's pronounced re-nig) or go back on our vow. For example, many people make New Year's resolutions to lose weight, eat healthier and exercise; but because we don't remain committed we soon "fall off the wagon".

We also make promises to others. For instance, we borrow money from someone and promise to pay them back in three months, but then six months roll around, and we get an attitude when they ask for THEIR money back! What ever happened to our word being our bond?

Also, couples exchange vows on their wedding day to love one another in sickness and in health, for richer or for poorer, for better or for worse, as long as they both shall live. Then one partner may become sick, gain weight, lose their job, or tell you two years later how unhappy they are, that the thrill is gone, and they want a divorce! How serious did they take those wedding vows from the beginning?

This following statement is sad but true. It's one thing to be married, and many people ARE. It's another thing to be married and happy, which many people ARE NOT. Far too often hundreds of people stay in loveless marriages because they don't want others to know just how unhappy and dysfunctional they really are behind closed doors, so they continue living a lie.

We also make promises to GOD, such as "Lord, if you get me out of this mess, I promise to live for you, all the days of my life". God soon finds out that our forever lasts only a short while.

But let the record show that our *awesome, loving* and *faithful* God **keeps** His promises! We can stand on the promises of God. Ezekiel 12:25a says: "For I am the Lord; I will speak, and the word that I shall speak **shall** come to pass; it shall no longer be prolonged or delayed".

II Corinthians 1:20, "For all the promises of God in him (*Jesus*) are yes and in him Amen unto the Glory of God by us" (*parentheses added*).

II Peter 1:4, "Whereby are given unto us (*make it personal and say unto ME*) exceeding great and precious promises" (*parentheses added*).

Romans 4:21, "And being fully persuaded that what He had promised, He was able also to perform".

Isaiah 41:10, "Fear not; for I am with you: be not dismayed; for I am your God: I will strengthen you: yes, I will help you: yes, I will uphold you with the right hand of my righteousness".

Dear Reader, it's **impossible** for God to lie! God is our refuge and strength, a very present help in time of trouble.

Romans 8:31, "What shall we say to these things? If God is for us, who can be against us?"

For those of you who have remained faithful to God, He promises to BLESS YOU. Your blessing is coming, it's on the way! Far too many times we become impatient waiting on God to bless us. We want it NOW, quick, fast and in a hurry!

Hebrews 10:36, "For **you** have need of patience, that **after** you have done the will of God, you might receive the promise". While you're waiting on the PROMISE, you must be willing to go through the PROCESS, to obtain the

PROMISE. There are some blessings God has just for YOU, but He knows you are not ready to handle them at this time. He's still working on your behalf. He wants you to be more mature, and He is deliberately placing people in your life who can help cultivate your gifts. God is a **promise keeper.**

When God gets ready to bless you, there is not a devil in hell that can stop Him from doing so! He doesn't have to ask permission from any board of directors, your friends, family, the Congress or the Senate. When God gets ready to bless you, the approval of others is not required! You ought to take a moment and shout, "Thank you Lord!"

God is still in the blessing business, and He can cause the blessings to chase you down, to overtake you, and cause showers of blessings to rain down upon you! God says the Greater One is already in you, if you're a child of God. That means you have greater possibilities, greater potential, greater power, greater favor, greater gifts, greater anointings. The Greater One promises to live in you, move in you, and to flow through you! So why are you fearful and doubting?

Don't you dare underestimate the precious promises of God, concerning YOU. He may not come when **you** want Him, but He will always be on time, and He will still be GOD when He gets there! That's a PROMISE.

3
MY CONDITION IS NOT MY CONCLUSION

The Woman with the Issue of Blood (Mark 5:25-34)

This is a story about a "certain woman". The verse does not personally give her a name, it just labels her as a "certain woman". In life many times people don't care about knowing your **name**, they only address you by your **shame** or your condition. This woman had an issue of blood for **TWELVE** years! An issue can also be interpreted as a problem or something you've been dealing or struggling with for a period of time. Let me start by saying that we **all** have issues! Family, health, financial, anger, emotional, relationship: they're ALL issues. And some of us have been dealing with our issues for a lot longer than twelve years!

In other words, this woman had been bleeding internally or hemorrhaging for twelve long years. That's 144 months, 624 weeks, 4,380 days and 8,760 hours that she experienced significant blood loss! Losing too much blood will leave a person very weak, dizzy, anemic, short of breath and they can also have irregular heartbeats, and headaches. Substantial blood loss can cause you to be vulnerable to other diseases and may even require blood transfusions. If not treated, it can be FATAL.

In verse 26 it says: "And she suffered MANY things of MANY physicians." Picture this woman for just a moment. There was no Obamacare, no Free Clinics, no Go Fund Me Accounts, No PPO's, Medicaid or Medicare. I'm sure her list of physicians included: her Primary care doctor, the Radiologist (X-rays), Gynecologist (female doctor), Hematologist (blood specialist), Oncologist (cancer doctor), not to mention all the co-pays, medications, and lab tests! She had spent ALL that she had. Now she was weaker, broke, discouraged and her condition was worse now than ever!

In verse 27, we read that when this woman heard of JESUS (*The Anointed One with the Anointing*), she made up her mind that *whatever it takes,* she was determined to get close to JESUS. This was a **desperate** woman, and desperate times calls for desperate measures. She "pressed" her way through the crowd and went to a place where she was NOT allowed! In those days a woman with a continuous flow of blood was considered unclean and filthy because of her "condition or issue". In spite of that, she was convinced that she had to get close to JESUS by any means necessary. Her very life was hanging in the balance. She simply had to seize this golden moment! Therefore, she **pressed** her way.

Have YOU ever had an urgency to press your way through? Perhaps you had to press your way past rejections, distractions, fears, tears, public opinions, judgmental people who try to demean, insult and shun you as though you were nothing more than a piece of gum stuck to the bottom of their shoe.

I'm certain that while this woman was "pressing" her way through the crowd, she had to mentally block out all the other people in the crowd. If she didn't get to JESUS expeditiously (*ASAP*), she could DIE. This "certain" woman wanted to LIVE! "For she said, 'If I can just touch his clothes, I shall be WHOLE (*healed*)'" (*Mark 5:28, capitalization and parentheses added for emphasis and understanding*). Another version of this same verse can be found in Matthew 9:20b which reads: "And behold a woman which was diseased with an issue of blood twelve years, came behind Him, and touched the **hem** of His garment."

There's something very significant about touching the **hem** of JESUS' garment. You see, when a tailor makes a garment, the last thing they sew is the **hem. The hem** represents a finished work! Just one touch from the Master can do more than all the earthly doctors, because of the "medicine" in the **hem** of His garment. I believe that someone reading this book needs to know RIGHT NOW, that there is Heavenly "medication" for your Earthly "situation".

Verse 29 says, "After she touched Him, the issue of blood was **suddenly** dried up!" That's because Jesus is a blood regulator. He specializes in HIGH Blood, LOW Blood and NO Blood at all! Yes, He is a Miracle Worker! This woman felt in her body that she was healed of that plague or "issue". Can you imagine how she must have felt after dealing with this condition for twelve long years, and to suddenly be healed? It makes me think of the words to an old hymn: "Something happened and now I know Jesus touched me and He made me whole".

Verse 30 says, "And Jesus immediately knew in himself that (*healing*) virtue had gone out of Him; so he turned to the multitude of people and said, 'Who touched my clothes?'" Has the Lord ever asked you a question, and you knew that He already knew the answer, but was testing your truthfulness?

Verse 31 reads: "And the disciples said unto Him, Lord you see all of these people gathered around you, and yet you ask the question "Who touched you?'" Jesus realized this was no ordinary touch. This was a touch of desperation. Of course, He already knew who touched

Him, because He is Omniscient (*all-knowing*). Yes, Jesus knows our ending from our beginning, He knows our thoughts before we think them, and He even knows the number of hairs on our head.

Verse 32 declares: "And He looked around the crowd to see the woman who had done this thing". Let me make something crystal clear: Jesus was not angry with this woman for touching Him. He already knew. Jesus asked the question in order to teach her something about FAITH.

Verse 33 says, "But the woman was fearful and trembling, realizing what she had done, and she humbled herself, fell down before Jesus and confessed what she did.

Verse 34 states: "And he said unto her, 'Daughter, your FAITH has made you whole; go in Peace and receive your healing!'" This woman's faith involved action! Faith that is not put into action is not faith at all. Hebrews 11:1 says, "NOW FAITH" (*sweetie, you need faith now, today*), "is the substance of things hoped for, the evidence of things not seen". In other words, you have to SEE it by FAITH before you actually receive it.

If you need a touch from the Lord, don't let "anything or anybody" hinder you from **pressing into His presence.** There is a BLESSING in your PRESSING! Once you enter into His presence, you will find joy, strength, love and peace. That's right! Jesus wants to give you real PEACE, so you won't fall into PIECES.

Activate your FAITH right now and confess that your condition is not your conclusion! I double dare you to shout: "The rest of my days shall be the best of my days!" Receive your healing, right now in JESUS' name!

J.R. Martinez

J.R. Martinez is a young vibrant, patriotic, ambitious and handsome man who served his country valiantly. When Martinez was 19 years old in the United States Army, he was stationed in Iraq, in 2003. His fellow soldier and friend ran over a land mine which caused a massive explosion, and J.R. found himself trapped inside of a Humvee (a military combat truck)! This young soldier suffered third degree burns on his body. His face was tragically scarred and disfigured.

Martinez remained in a coma for three weeks. He was unable to walk, bathe or feed himself. This was a very traumatic circumstance for such a young person. Because of all the scarring, skin grafts, and excruciating pain caused by the accident, J.R. became bitter for a while. I'm certain he asked the Lord, "Why Me?" Don't you think **you** would do the same in that situation? However, he soon came to realize that a positive attitude could actually help to expedite his healing process.

He was very blessed to have a loving, caring, supportive and praying mother! He reassured and comforted his mother, by telling her one way or another he was coming back home to the United States of America. As we have seen, the Bible says in Hebrew 11:1, "Now FAITH, is the substance of things **hoped for**, the evidence of things **not seen"**. Real faith is "knowing" that God is able to do the impossible in your life, and He "will" see you through. Beloved, you too must realize that your words have POWER. Life and death are in the power of your tongue. Learn to speak LIFE to your circumstances, your situations and your challenges.

Over the next three years J.R. endured 33 operations and had to painfully suffer through skin debridement, due to the severity of his burns. This young soldier suffered public humiliation. People stared, pointed, and out of ignorance called him all types of degrading names. Yet he was determined that things were going to get better. He believed that there was a light at the end of this dark tunnel. He believed that **his condition was not his conclusion.**

In spite of all the hurt and pain that Martinez endured. He used this experience to help raise awareness about the dangers and casualties service members face on a regular basis.

J.R. credits his recovery to his single mother, who loved her son unconditionally, because she knew he was still beautiful on the inside. She was just grateful that her child was still alive. She knew that he was a survivor and a thrive*r*!

Despite J.R.'s disfigurement from the war, he became an actor, motivational speaker, and he even graced the cover of People Magazine! I was one of his biggest fans when he became a contestant on the popular television program, "Dancing with the Stars". He was very smooth and agile on the dance floor and, in 2011, he won the coveted "Mirror Ball Trophy". J.R. **refused** to let his **condition** become his **conclusion.** I personally watched him on the show "every" Monday night, and I phoned in my votes!

To top it all off, Martinez fell in love with a beautiful woman who loved him and was not disgusted or turned off by his physical scars. She must have realized that beauty is only skin deep! J.R. is also the proud father of a darling daughter named Lauryn Anabelle Martinez. What an awesome and powerful legacy to leave with his daughter to cherish! Can't you just imagine this father telling his daughter, **"I don't look like what I've been through!"**

4
IT'S NOT OVER UNTIL GOD SAYS IT'S OVER

Let's focus on the story of Job. In the first chapter, it says "There was a man in the land of Uz, whose name was Job; and he was a perfect and upright man who feared God and avoided evil" (see Job 1:1). He had ten children, seven sons and three daughters. Job was a very wealthy man who took his relationship with the Lord seriously. He prayed daily over his children, even after they reached adulthood. What an admirable trait for a loving father!

"Now there was a day when the sons of God came to present themselves before the Lord, and Satan (the devil) came also among them" (Job 1:6). Isn't that just like Satan today, you go to church to hear and receive the word, to be blessed, and here comes the devil with a lot of mess!

In verses 7-12, Satan and the Lord are actually having a conversation about Job. "The Lord said unto Satan, 'Have you considered my servant Job, that there is none like him in the earth, a perfect and an upright man, one who fears God and shuns the appearance of evil?'" (Job 1:8)

Think of this verse as though God himself was "bragging" on Job. You, dear Reader, just might be a modern-day Job! The Lord might be having a conversation with Satan asking him "Have you considered my servant _____ (insert your name here)? The word "consider" means to pay close attention to before making a decision. Could it be that YOU are being considered for a trial or test, and God is "bragging" on you? Not because you're perfect, but God's bragging on you because He is confident in what He's placed on the **inside** of YOU. The Lord already knows there is **greatness, potential, integrity, strength** and **faithfulness** down on the inside of YOU.

Beloved, you will never realize the depth of the resilience that God has deposited in you, until you've been tested! The Lord has a great investment in you, just as He did with Job.

Job wound up losing all ten of his children! He also lost servants and livestock after a great wind **suddenly** hit his children's home, where they were eating and drinking wine. All ten of his children were killed!

Now let's be **real**. Have you ever wondered why bad things happen to good and godly people? Have you ever thought, "Why would God allow His people to suffer?" I know that **I** have!

II Timothy 3:12 states: "Yes, and **all** that will live godly in Christ Jesus **shall** suffer persecution". Persecution is when you are being pursued and constantly afflicted especially for religious reasons. Psalm 34:19 says: "**Many** (not any, but MANY) are the afflictions of the righteous: but the Lord delivers us out of them all".

Job's situation lets us know that even though we may be Christians, that does **not** exempt us from going through trials, tests, storms or challenges. Beloved, it doesn't matter if you are called, chosen, anointed and appointed; your faith will still be tested. You can have more degrees behind your name than a thermometer, talk in tongues, interpret tongues, be a bishop over twelve churches, be the CEO of a major company, preach like Bishop Jakes or sing like Tamela Mann, the devil will still try to attack you by any means necessary! You may even pay your tithes and offerings faithfully, and be in church every time the doors open, but you will still have some valley experiences and some seasons of midnight. If you don't believe me, "keep on living".

Satan replied to God by saying: "Stretch forth your hand and take away everything that Job has, and he will curse you to your face" (see Job 1:11). What Satan really meant was if God removed the hedge of protection around Job, he would no longer serve God. Evidently Satan assumed that Job had "superficial faith" and was only serving God for the "perks". However, "real faith" is strengthened by life's adversities!

Yes, Job was righteous and holy, but he was also human. He was truly devastated by the loss of his ten children! Let's consider some of us. Maybe you don't know how it feels to work hard all of your life to get what you have and come home one day to find your home engulfed in flames with your family members trapped inside and **suddenly** all of your loved ones and priceless possessions are charred ruins. And all you have left are mixed emotions and bitter-sweet memories. When things happen **suddenly** and unexpectedly in life, they catch you totally off guard!

Lately on the news, we hear of many people who have been devastated by floods, hurricanes, wild fires, mud slides, road rage, domestic violence, mass murders and school shootings! These types of **sudden** tragedies can literally knock the wind out of the strongest of people! Have YOU ever felt that there seemed to be so many troubles and storms in your personal life building up until you were overcome by an avalanche or tsunami of problems, that you thought they would literally take you OUT of here? I'm sure Job felt that same way.

In addition to losing his ten children, all of his cattle and livestock, his friends turned on him when he needed them most, and boils broke out all over Job's body. His physical appearance changed so much because of the boils and weight loss that his friends and servants no longer recognized him! Even though Job was a righteous man, he sank into a pit of severe depression. If you don't believe it, read it for yourself in the third chapter of Job.

Job's friends, or should I say his "frenemies" (those fake, phony and pretentious ones who say one thing to your face and another behind your back), assumed he had sinned because of all that he was going through. They didn't have a clue! Believe it or not, there are some people in your family, and even some people you call your friends, who think YOU have sinned and are being punished by God. The truth is they really don't have a clue about what you're going through!

Mrs. Job enters the picture in Job 2:9, when she says to her husband, "Why are you still holding on to your integrity (moral uprightness)?" She also says, "Just curse God and die!" Satan often will use the people closest to us to cause us to question or doubt God's heart toward us and we begin to think, "Why even bother praying or holding on to our confession of faith, when God has allowed all of this heartache to happen?" Mrs. Job felt "death" would be better than seeing her husband go through so much pain and anguish!

Let's not be too quick to point a judgmental finger at Job's wife for her remarks. Have YOU ever said things that you later regretted? I believe her words were spoken out of despair and bitterness. After all, she saw her life collapse before her very eyes also. She was consumed with grief. Her heart was overwhelmed!

It's one thing to lose a parent or spouse, but it's altogether different when you lose a child, regardless of their age. No loving parent wants to outlive their children. I'm sure that Mrs. Job wondered why she and her husband's lives were spared, and not their children. None of us have all of the answers we desire to all of our questions. The human side of us is prone to ask, "Why Lord", "Why ME?" "How long must I go through this?"

Picture this in your compassionate mind: Mrs. Job gave birth to ten children! That means she experienced strange food cravings, swollen ankles, stretch marks, and LABOR PAINS. All she had left were the memories of breast feeding, burping, singing lullabies, reading bedtime stories as she rocked her babies to sleep. I'm sure she thought of all the thousands of diapers that had to be changed over the years. She cleaned up poop, puke and pee, cleaned runny noses, put Band-Aids on "boo-boos". I'm sure she taught her children how to say grace before eating and their prayers at night, before going to bed.

I just believe that her mind was inundated with her children's FIRSTS: the first time she held them in her arms after giving birth, their first teeth, words, steps; their first day at school, first date, prom, as well as their first broken heart. She was a proud mother when her first daughter was escorted down the aisle by Job to give his daughter's hand in marriage. Can't you just picture this mother training her children up in the way that they should go, teaching them to respect themselves, others and to put God first. I'm sure she taught them how to save for a rainy day. Let's "cut Mrs. Job some slack"! Even though they had hired servants, I think she also taught her children how to get the most out of a "chicken!" She fried it, stewed it, baked, broiled, boiled and barbecued it! Nothing on that "bird" was going to waste, because you could make sandwiches and chop it up for chicken salad. You saw that meat for DAYS, but it was prepared in different WAYS. They ate and were full or were told (if they were "picky eaters") "You'll eat it before it eats YOU".

Suddenly, Mr. and Mrs. Job find themselves at a Funeral Home, picking out not one but TEN caskets to bury their children, while gathering information for the obituaries through tear-filled eyes! I can only imagine the insurmountable and devastating grief the two of them must have felt. Let the record show that we "all" handle grief differently. Precious Reader, there is no blueprint for the right or wrong way to grieve.

There Are Five Stages of Grief:

Grief is an intense emotional suffering caused by loss or disaster. It's a normal emotion. Grief means to feel sadness sorrow or distress. We all handle grief differently.

The first stage of grief is DENIAL/SHOCK. A death has actually happened. It has no set time frame. People in denial often withdraw from normal social behavior and become isolated. The person has a hard time dealing with the loss of their loved one or may feel as if it's a really bad dream!

The second stage of grief is ANGER/FRUSTRATION. People who are grieving sometimes become angry with the person or situation which caused them to be in this predicament. Many become angry and bitter towards God for allowing the death to happen. They may even refuse to go to church or read the Bible, as a form of revenge against God. They are angry that their hopes have been crushed and their prayers were not answered as they anticipated. They feel as though God has let them down, just as Martha did when she said to Jesus in John 11:21, "Lord, if you had been here, my brother wouldn't be dead".

The third stage of grief is BARGAINING/ STRUGGLING to find the reasons WHY. The grieving person is looking for ways to help ease the pain they are feeling, and make it disappear. Some people will try and make a deal or promise to do whatever it takes to have their pain removed.

The fourth stage of grief is DEPRESSION/FEELING OVERWHELMED. This raw emotion usually sets in when you finally realize your loved one is really gone. Periods of depression can vary with each person. It helps if you don't spend all of your time focusing on how your loved one died, but on how they lived! You can choose to give up or go on.

The fifth stage of grief is ACCEPTANCE. Acceptance is the beginning of the inner healing process. It takes place when you are no longer consumed with mourning on a constant basis. It's the point in time where recovery becomes about the person left behind and not about the person being mourned. You can now reflect on the happy and precious memories that you shared with your loved one.

Even Mr. and Mrs. Job had to deal with these five stages of grief. Nevertheless, there is a wonderful ending to the story of Job. Thank God, "Job's condition was not his CONCLUSION". There was light at the end of the tunnel for him. His troubles had an EXPIRATION date. His troubles didn't last always! In the 42nd chapter of Job, verse 10, it states: "The Lord turned the captivity of Job when he prayed for his friends" (*or frenemies: the very ones who smiled in his face, and called him everything but a child of God, behind his back*); "also the Lord gave Job twice as much as he had before." In other words, he got DOUBLE for all his TROUBLE! Let's keep it real. It's not easy forgiving and praying for someone who has lied on you and accused you of wrong doing; but Job did. Are YOU able to follow Job's example and forgive people who have done you wrong? In life, we can't always control what happens to us, but we can control how we react.

Dear Reader, for ALL that you've been through, God has a blessing with YOUR name on it! What God has for YOU, it is for YOU! You don't have to wait until the battle is over, you can shout HALLELUJAH right NOW! The enemy wants you to think things will never get any better for you. He wants you to think that you are having a BREAK-DOWN, But, you need to open up your mouth and say MY BREAK-THROUGH is on the way! My God is turning things around for me! My God is turning things around for MY GOOD. The REST of my days, shall be the BEST of my days! The devil thought you were down for the count, but there was a "bounce back" in your spirit! Old Satan, with his stupid self, thought he was going to give the benediction over your life...But God said, "Your CURRENT is not your PERMANENT", and this CONDITION is NOT your CONCLUSION!!

It's Not Over Until God Says It's Over

How Hannah Got Her Joy Back

Sometimes in our lives we may be faced with some tests and challenges that seem to be so unfair and unbearable. In the Old Testament book of I Samuel, beginning in the first chapter, we find a story about a woman named Hannah, whose Hebrew name means "Grace". In those days polygamy (having more than one wife) was permissible. A man named Elkanah had two wives, Hannah and Peninnah. Peninnah was very fertile and was able to have children, but Hannah was barren, because the Lord had "shut up" her womb! Keep in mind that anything that God "shuts up", He is able to open in His divine timing. We don't always understand God's ways or His timing!

Hannah **desperately** wanted to have children and being unable to conceive caused her to totally lose her JOY. In Old Testament times a childless woman was considered a failure and an embarrassment to her husband. By law, he could even divorce her. Hannah knew in her heart that her husband loved her, but even his love could not comfort her nor fill the void in her life. To add insult to injury, Hannah was being constantly provoked and ridiculed by her husband's other wife, Peninnah. It seemed as though every time Hannah turned around, Peninnah was pregnant! I can imagine Peninnah saying things to Hannah, such as: "Girl, just look at my swollen ankles, will you get me a couple of pillows to prop my legs up". Or, "Elkanah's baby is kicking me hard right now, do you want to feel my stomach?" With her insensitive self, I can even imagine Peninnah saying, "I was craving dill pickles and butter pecan ice cream last night, and you already know that our "boo" went and got it for me! When you're a **real** woman, there's no limit to what a man will do for you!

Hannah just couldn't take this woman and her insults any longer! Her JOY was gone. Hannah realized if her JOY was going to be restored, there were three things that she needed to do.

1. She had to **PRESS** her way. To "press" means to do what you really don't feel like doing, until you feel like doing it! This was a test for Hannah, and without a **test,** there can be no **testimony.** Sometimes you may have to press **your** way! Press through the hurts, pains, oppositions, and even press your way through the tears streaming down your face. Hannah pressed her way to the house of God! For it's in the House of God where we find refuge, anticipate being in the presence of the Lord and hearing a word from Him. Hannah had become so discouraged and depressed that she lost her appetite, lost a lot of weight, and couldn't seem to stop crying, all because of her situation. But deep within she believed she was in the right place to have her needs met. She really wanted her JOY back, but realized she had to take another step.

2. She had to **PRAY.** She had to call on the name that's above every other name! Dear Reader, when we call on the name of JESUS, something supernatural begins to happen. **P-** Pray **U-** Until **S-** Something **H-** Happens. **(PUSH).** Verse 10 of I Samuel says: "She (Hannah) was in bitterness of soul and prayed unto the Lord, crying uncontrollably." In other words, she was a desperate woman and desperate times call for desperate measures! She was not trying to pray a cute and rehearsed prayer. This woman of God was praying from the recesses of her soul! As she was praying, Eli the priest was sitting upon a seat by the post of the temple observing Hannah. He saw her lips moving, but was unable to hear what she was saying, so he assumed she was drunk. Far too many "church folks" are quick to jump to conclusions and try to judge you, when they really don't have a clue! If the truth were to be told, sometimes we are just too **nosey**; we're all up in somebody's Kool-Aid and don't even know the flavor. Here we have Hannah pouring out her heart and soul to the Lord, and Eli the priest asked her in Verse 14, "How long will you keep getting drunk? Get rid of your wine!" Yes, even preachers can get off track and miss God!

In Verse 15, Hannah answered Eli and said, "I am a deeply troubled woman and I have **not** had any alcoholic beverages. I'm here in the House of God, praying that I will get a **breakthrough,** before I have a **break-down**".

Hannah made a vow to the Lord, that if He blessed her with a son, she would dedicate him to the Lord all the days of his life. After listening to Hannah's real testimony, Eli the priest told her to go in **peace** (not pieces) and that the Lord would grant the request she asked of Him, because she had found Grace in God's sight. Now it's time for Hannah's third and final step.

3. She had to *PRAISE.* When Hannah left the temple she was no longer sad, her countenance (facial expression) changed and her appetite returned, because God had finally turned things around for her! She didn't have a break-down, because God gave her a mighty **breakthrough!** She didn't leave the house of God, the same way that she came! The joy bells were ringing in her soul. The clapping returned to her hands, and the dancing returned to her feet! A great change had come over Hannah. When she went home and laid with her husband Elkanah, this time she conceived and had a son whom she named Samuel, saying, "because I asked him of the Lord". She did not forget the vow that she made unto the Lord! In Verses 26-28, Hannah said, "O my Lord, I am the woman that stood here praying. I prayed for this child, and you granted my request, therefore as long as he lives he shall be yours".

This is the place where Hannah really gets her JOY back! In I Samuel 2:1-2, "And Hannah prayed, and said, 'My heart rejoices in the Lord, He has made me strong, my mouth speaks boldly against my enemies, because I rejoice in your salvation. There is absolutely nobody as holy as the Lord, for no one else anywhere can begin to compare to the Lord. There's nobody like Him! Neither is there any rock like MY GOD.'" This is a good place for another PRAISE break!

For when I think of His goodness, and all He's done for me, when I think of His goodness and how He set ME free, I can dance, dance, dance all night!!

*****

It doesn't matter how dark and gloomy your life may appear to be, or what you may have lost that was near and dear to you, your life is not over, until **God** says it's over! Even if your enemies and frenemies (those pretending to be your real friends) are plotting, scheming and trying to dig ditches for you to fall in, they'd better be really careful, because the ditch they dig just might be for "them".

Even if a team of doctors say that they've done all they can do and recommend that your immediate family come in and say their final "good-byes" to you, let the records show that there is another doctor named Dr. Jesus, who is the Great Physician, and **HE** has the final say so over your life! Beloved, every sickness is **not** unto death!

If the skeptics and naysayers assume you will never make it **out** of your current situation, I want you to know if there's a way **in** it, there's a way **out** of it, and **JESUS is the WAY!** Oh yes, He is still a way maker, and He has already given your problems an expiration date and made a way for your escape!

Sometimes when we are going through, we may feel as though God is nowhere (to be found). But I challenge you to look at the word "nowhere" through the eyes of faith and realize that God is **now here!** Yes, He is Jehovah-Shammah, which means the LORD is there (for YOU)!

Isaiah 41 verse 10 says: "Fear not, for I am with you; Be not dismayed, for I am your God. I will strengthen you, Yes I will help you". Whenever GOD says He **will** do something, that's His blessed assurance to us that He will do just what He said! When you need Him the most, He **will** step right in the midst of your situation, in time and on time! That's because God has the final say so over your life, and it's not over until **GOD** says it's over!

Beloved Reader, don't you DARE try and place a **period,** where God places a **comma** (in your life). The period represents the **ending** of a sentence. The **comma** indicates it's not the **ending** of a sentence, it implies that there is **more to come.** If you don't try to miss this gem, you will get it! Marinate on it. In other words, your life is **not over** because you are still alive to read the words on this page.

Your life is not a done deal YET. It's not finished, it's not over! You may get knocked down, but you have not been knocked out! You may be bent, but you are not broken! Others, including yourself if you are to be honest, may think that your time has passed, but I want you to know that GOD is saving the **best** for **last.** You must believe that your future is brighter and better than your past. Your worst days are behind you, and your best days are ahead of you! Your latter shall be greater than your past! Your condition is **not** your conclusion. What you started with is not what you're stuck with! So, don't you dare give up on GOD, because GOD has **not** given up on YOU!

Since death and life are in the power of **your** tongue, why don't you open your mouth right now, and speak over your own life, and boldly declare: "I don't look like, what I've been through!" "My problems do not define my purpose!" "What I started with, is not what I'm stuck with!" "My history does not determine my destiny!" "I believe that God is for me, and right now I believe that God is leaning in my direction, and this is MY SEASON and MY TIME TO BE BLESSED!" "I believe that GOD has spared my life for such a time as THIS", and "Since I'm still here, still alive and I'm still standing, I owe GOD the praise, the Glory and all the Honor". "Because of GOD and His Son

Jesus Christ, MY FAITH has been renewed, MY JOY has been restored, MY DOUBTS have been replaced with FAITH, strongholds have been pulled down, BURDENS have been removed, SHACKLES have fallen off, CHAINS have been broken, YOKES have been destroyed, all because of the ANOINTING!"

I personally found out that my situations should **not** affect or change my PRAISE, but my PRAISE can definitely affect and change my situations! You ought to join me right now and let us make the devil steaming mad by throwing our heads back, by raising our hands towards heaven, by leaping for JOY, and shouting from the top of our lungs, **"I'm so glad that it's not over until GOD says it's over! God is the God of another chance. He brought me out, over and through!"**

NOW GO AHEAD AND TAKE YOURSELF A RADICAL PRAISE BREAK!!

P.S. "Your PRAISE will totally confuse your enemy."

5
GOD IS ABLE TO TURN IT AROUND

It doesn't matter how bad your circumstance or situation may seem, you have to know in your heart and have faith that God is Omnipotent (has all power). He is well able to **reverse** the **adverse** in your life. What the enemy intended for your harm, God can turn it around for your good and for His Glory.

GOD CAN TURN:

A Negative	into	A Positive
Midnight	into	Morning
Darkness	into	Light
Trials	into	Triumphs
Poverty	into	Wealth
Addiction	into	Deliverance

God is Up to Something Concerning YOU

A Victim	into	A Victor
Stumbling Blocks	into	Stepping Stones
Fear	into	Faith
Hurts	into	Healings
Lack	into	Abundance
Pressure	into	Praise
Sickness	into	Health
Weakness	into	Strength
Brokenness	into	Wholeness
Devastation	into	Restoration
A Mess	into	A Message
A Test	into	A Testimony
Misery	into	Ministry
Your History	into	Your Destiny

God Is Able to Turn It Around

Pitiful	into	Powerful
Problems	into	Possibilities
Broken Pieces	into	Master Pieces
Famine	into	Fulfillment
The Forgotten	into	The Favored
A Prostitute	into	A Prophetess
Worry	into	Worship
An Outcast	into	An Overcomer
Your Set-back	into	Your Come-back

6
A NOTICE TO SATAN

ATTENTION SATAN:

You have been loosed of your assignment against me.

Your plans, tricks and schemes have been revealed.

Your strategies have been exposed.

You have already been stripped of your position in Heaven.

I know you want to steal, kill and destroy me by any means necessary.

You want to assassinate my character, mutilate my reputation, annihilate my praise, and steal my joy.

YOU are a defeated foe. You no longer possess the power to depress, oppress or suppress me. I don't belong to you anymore.

A Notice to Satan

You are no longer my master, and I am no longer a slave to sin.

I am under new management, and you are now a trespasser. You have been issued an eviction notice.

Your satanic attacks against me have been rendered helpless, powerless, defeated, null and void.

The Greater One is living in me now, and Greater is He that is in me than he that is in the world.

No, I'm not perfect, but I serve a perfect God who is perfecting all of my imperfections.

My sins have been forgiven and I'm covered in the Blood of Jesus Christ.

Your fiery darts will not consume or burn me, because no weapon formed against me shall prosper.

I know you desire to sift me as wheat, but I'm coming through the sifting process better, stronger and wiser than ever before.

I am equipped with the whole armor of God. The weapons of my warfare are not carnal, but MIGHTY through God, to the pulling down of your strongholds.

I belong to God, from the crown of my head to the soles of my feet.

I am the head and not the tail. I am above only and not beneath.

I'm not a loser, I'm a winner. I am now a saint and not a sinner.

I serve an AWESOME GOD.

I believe the report of the Lord. His report says I am forgiven, blessed, healed, loved, loosed, delivered and totally set free!

I am more than a conqueror through Christ who loves me.

My history does not abort my destiny.

This is not "Fake News" Satan.

God said it, that settles it, whether you believe it or not.

Unapologetically,
A Child of the King

7
WHAT I START WITH IS NOT WHAT I'M STUCK WITH

You may wonder why I chose to write about Steve Harvey, of all people. Let me be bold enough to tell you why. First of all, he doesn't **look like** what he's been through. In spite of the fact that Mr. Harvey is very well known for his "colorful language" or **cussing**, I still chose to write about him.

Let me say to any religious "fault finders" that may read this writing, "Please don't **accuse** in others, what you **excuse** in yourself". Frankly speaking, I know a lot of preachers who can literally preach the screws out of the pews, and then curse/cuss you out over a parking space! "IJS." (I'm just saying).

None of us have reached perfection yet, we are all a W.I.P. (work in progress). In other words, we are a piece of unfinished work. The Potter is still molding the clay (us). God still has to "tweak, change and delete some things from our lives in order for Him to get the ultimate glory.

Steve would be the first to admit that he is still on the Potter's Wheel, and God is not through with him yet.

However, I heard and saw Mr. Harvey give one of the most stirring, spirit-filled and captivating introductions of who **Jesus Christ** is in a way that I've never witnessed before or since. Even "seasoned" preachers were in awe of his rendition.

While Steve was waiting on his "breakthrough" in life, he was not idle, because he worked numerous jobs. He also slept in his car, went without food, was given clothes to wear because he couldn't afford to buy any. His success did not happen overnight. That should let you know that in this life, you too will encounter some adversities, but if you hold on and keep the faith, your breakthrough will surely come!

In the urban community Steve is called "blue cheese", because of his stylish **dressing**. Even now, he attributes his flair for dressing to Mr. Albert's Men's Store in Cleveland, Ohio.

The point that I'm trying to make is that his **future** was NOT erased because of his **past**. As a child he knew that one day his name would be great! One of his brothers said that Steve made a sign and placed it over his bedroom door that read: "One day I'm going to make a million dollars!"

What I Start with Is Not What I'm Stuck With

Could it be that as a child Steve was calling those things that be not as though they were? In this journey called life, it may seem as though the odds may be stacked against you, and even though your situation may look or seem impossible, will **you** still dare to chase after your dreams? Will **you** still trust God, when doors are closed in your face?

Steve's road to success was an uphill journey. He made plenty of mistakes and regrets some of the choices he made. Nevertheless, he continued to pursue his passions. One thing that I admire about Steve is his "challenge" to us to **never** give up on our dreams!

Dear Reader, are **you** still pursuing your passions in life? Let me ask you another question: What is the one thing in life you enjoy doing so much, that if you were unable to ever do it again, your life would be most miserable? Is your passion so great, that even if you were not paid, you would still want to do it?

Because of Mr. Harvey's experiences, trials and even failures, he believes once you become successful, you **must** pay it forward! His mantra is: "There is no way you can see people struggling and don't do anything about it, when it's in your power to help".

Not only does Steve believe this, but the Bible says in I John 3:17, "If anyone has material possessions and sees someone in **need, (not greed)**, and shows no pity or compassion for them, how can the love of God be in you?" After all, we are blessed to be a blessing!

Some of Steve's greatest accomplishments include being the host of Show Time at the Apollo for seven years (1993-2000). He is one of the "Original Kings of Comedy", a best-selling author, an actor, comedian and entertainer. He has a mentoring camp for young boys where he and 60 other men, including blue collar workers and successful men from various professions, give of their time, wisdom and expertise, by "pouring" into these young men's lives. After all, it takes a village to raise a child.

Many of these young men have no father figures in their lives, so they are taught how to respect themselves and others, how to be gentlemen, the importance of a good education, taking pride in earning honest money and how to manage it, and to always remember, "With God, all things are possible!" (see Matthew 19:26)

Steve has a Men's Fragrance Soap, a clothing line, an Easy Bacon line that includes "chocolate bacon". He is also the host of his own Talk Show, Radio Show, Family Feud, Funderdome, Forever Young and Little Big Shots.

What I Start with Is Not What I'm Stuck With

Wow! That ought to convince you that your **condition** is not your **conclusion,** and **what you start with, is not what you're stuck with!**

Let me close this chapter by saying that challenges and failures are necessary components for **success.** Your failure can actually become a bridge to your success. Failure can be a success if you learn from it. Remember, just because you fail once, doesn't mean you will fail at everything. If you refuse to quit when you fail, eventually you too will be successful!

8
WISE SAYINGS

You are not a waste of space.

Don't try to make sense out of nonsense.

Don't put all your eggs into one basket.

A penny saved is a penny earned.

Don't count your chickens before they hatch.

What strikes the oyster shell does not damage the pearl.

Wherever you find people, you'll find problems.

People may not believe what you "say" you do, but they will believe what they "see" you do.

Actions speak louder than words.

A tree is known by the fruit it bears.

Wise Sayings

People don't care how much you know until they know how much you care.

You are what you repeatedly do.

Even a fish would not get in trouble if he kept his mouth closed.

Your history does not determine your destiny.

Positive thinking produces positive results.

Birds of a feather flock together.

You are known by the company you keep.

People are your friends because of what you have in common.

We teach people how to treat us.

Oh, what a tangled web we weave, when first we practice to deceive.

If you always do what you've always done, you'll always be where you've always been.

Our choices have consequences.

Whoever you're connected to, you'll be affected by.

The same boiling water that hardens the egg, softens the potato.

People who have nothing to hide, hide nothing.

When people "show" you who they are, believe them.

Winners are not people who never fail, but winners are people who never quit.

God gave us two ears and one mouth for a reason.

Everything that glitters isn't gold.

A family that prays together stays together.

9
I DON'T LOOK LIKE WHAT I'VE BEEN THROUGH

Tamar (not Tamar Braxton)

In the Old Testament, in the Book of II Samuel the 13th chapter, is an interesting story about family dysfunction and incest (sexual intercourse between people who are closely related). David is the king of Jerusalem at this time and he has a lot of children by many different women. Any time you have children by multiple women, there's bound to be some "baby mama drama".

Let's take a real close look at this story, which could actually be on reality TV. In verse 1, it states that David's son Absalom had a very beautiful sister named **Tamar,** and Amnon, the son of David, loved her. Amnon was Tamar's step-brother, and the love he had for her was actually **lust!**

In verse 2, Amnon was so frustrated because he wanted to have sex with Tamar. Every time he saw her, he fantasized. The Bible declares in Matthew 5:28, "Whoever looks on a woman to lust (to feel an intense sexual desire that you want satisfied) after her, has committed **adultery** with her already in his heart!" Amnon knew that Tamar was a virgin, that she was his half-sister, and therefore off-limits; yet he still struggled with his emotions.

In verse 3, Amnon had a friend/ first cousin, whose name was Jonadab, his father David's nephew. Jonadab was very **subtle** (conniving, cunning, manipulative).

In verse 4, Jonadab said unto his cousin Amnon, "You're the king's son, what's going on with you? You're losing too much weight" I am paraphrasing this line: Cousin, you're looking a **hot mess**, now tell me what's really going on!" Finally, Amnon replied, "I love **Tamar**, my brother Absalom's sister".

In verse 5, Jonadab is giving his cousin some ungodly advice. Beloved, you better be real careful from whom **you** receive advice or counseling! Psalm 1:1a says "Blessed is the man that walks **not** in the counsel of the ungodly".

Jonadab told Amnon to lay upon his bed and make himself sick! In other words, pretend to be sick, as the young people say in our time: perpetrate a fraud! He also added, "When your dad comes to see you, tell him how terrible and weak you feel. Plead with him by asking for Tamar to come and take care of you, and nurse you back to health." Does this scenario sound like a "scheming demon" to you?

In verses 6 and 7, Amnon follows through with the scheme, and evidently, he was quite convincing because King David told Tamar to go immediately to Amnon's and prepare him something to eat.

In verse 8, we see that out of obedience to her father, David, this innocent and vulnerable young woman went to her half-brother's home, not realizing that she was being "set-up". Tamar made the special cakes that Amnon requested.

In verses 9 and 10, after she went through the process of baking the cakes, and attempting to serve them to Amnon, he **refused** to eat! He had a hidden agenda from the very start. He then commanded that all of his servants leave the room immediately! Afterwards, Amnon instructed Tamar to bring the food into his bedroom, so she could privately feed him without interruptions.

In verse 11, when she brought the food for him to eat, he **grabbed** her and said, "Come lie with me, my sister". How **appalling!** But this type of perversion has been going on for a long time! Read the story for yourself in Genesis 19:30-38, where Lot's two daughters got him drunk and had sex with their own father, and then justified the act by saying his seed would be preserved. The Jerry Springer Show has nothing on this true story.

In verse 12, Tamar responded by saying, **"No my brother, do not force me. Please don't do this wicked thing to me"**. She goes on to say that "such a thing should NOT be done in Israel". She is pleading, fearful and trembling!

In verse 13, she knows that her brother is going to RAPE her, so she pleads with him, "What about ME? Where would I be able to go and get rid of this disgrace and shame?" "And what about YOU? You would be like one of the wicked fools in Israel. If you ask the king for my hand in marriage, he will probably allow it, but PLEASE don't rape me!"

In verse 14, he (Amnon) refused to listen to her, and since he was stronger than Tamar, he RAPED her. He sexually abused her! Let me enlighten you about sexual abuse/assault. It includes any type of sexual contact or conduct with another person, without their permission, that's **not** consensual. It's a violation that includes RAPE, INCEST, DATE RAPE, GANG RAPE, MARITAL RAPE, and MOLESTATION. Let the records show that **sexual abuse is not about sexual gratification, it's about power and control.**

In verse 15, then Amnon **hated her exceedingly**; so that the hatred with which he **hated her was greater than the love he had for her.** That emotion was not love at all, it was 100% **lust.** And after he violated Tamar, he cold-heartedly told her to "get up and GO!" He discarded her like a piece of trash, because he no longer desired her, and was repulsed at her presence. Yes, he demanded her to get out of his bed, bedroom and his sight! He threw her under the bus and kicked her to the curb!

In verse 16, she said unto him, "sending me away like **this**, would be a greater wrong than what you've already done to me!" But he would not listen to her. By throwing Tamar out, Amnon made it seem as though she had made a shameful proposition to him, and there were no witnesses to validate her version of the story, because he had gotten rid of his servants. His crime destroyed her chances of marriage. Because she was no longer a virgin, she could not be given in marriage; she was forever tainted.

In verse 17, he called his personal servant and said, "Get this woman out of here **now**, and lock the door behind her!" Now this was cold-blooded and ruthless, wouldn't you agree?

In verse 18, Tamar was wearing a richly ornamented robe of many colors, because this was the kind of garment that virgin daughters of the king wore.

In verse 19, Tamar put ashes on her head (ashes were used as a sign of grief and humiliation). She tore the ornamented robe she was wearing. She put her hand on her head and went away, weeping uncontrollably! Her brother Absalom said to her, "Has that Amnon, **your brother,** been with you? Be quiet my sister; he is your brother, don't turn this incident into a public scandal" Doesn't that remind you of the phrase, "What happens in Vegas, stays in Vegas", or "What happens in this house, stays in this house?"

All too often many people of sexual abuse are victimized all over again. Even people in their own family accuse them of "wanting it", or say the victim walked the wrong way, acted the wrong way, or dressed inappropriately. There are countless numbers of young children who are being "groomed" by their sexual predators on a daily basis. The offender gains their trust, before stealing their innocence, and emotionally scarring them for life. These perverted offenders are rarely strangers, more often than not, they are "trusted" family members, friends of the family, teachers and sadly even some clergy.

The media has recently brought a lot of attention to the **"ME TOO MOVEMENT".** Many celebrities, athletes and entertainers are coming forward to expose their abusers, and letting the world know that they will no longer live in **silence or shame.** I personally applaud the

Grammy winning Gospel singer and Pastor Donnie McClurkin for being so transparent in talking about how he was sexually violated, raped and molested by his uncle at the innocent age of eight, and then by that uncle's son, at the age of thirteen. He wrote a book about it, and even showed the pictures. He did that for his own healing, and to let others know they are not alone, nor do they have to suffer in silence.

Even Oprah and Tyler Perry have shared their stories of being molested as children. This epidemic is happening more often than we know, considering the fact that many who have been violated, will never share their stories, and suffer in silence. If you or someone you know, is the victim of sexual abuse, please don't suffer in silence any longer. Get help! There is help available where you can remain anonymous. There are trained people who specialize in helping hurting, broken and confused victims with counseling sessions. They can also assist them in reclaiming their value and self-worth, so they can go on to live productive lives. Most importantly, the counselors can teach them how to go from being a **victim** to becoming a **victor and a survivor!** Oprah survived her sexual abuse, and she is now one of the most recognizable and richest women in the world.

God has truly turned Donnie McClurkin's **mess** into his **message.** If you've never heard his song STAND, please take time to listen to the words of this survivor!

Tyler Perry aka "Madea", makes millions of us laugh, even though he was also sexually abused as a young person, by men and women. He internalized his pain for years. Finally, he decided to turn his **pain** into **praise.** Believe me when I say, "you're **not** the only one!

Before I close this chapter, let's look at verse 20 of II Samuel 13. Secretly, Absalom planned to take revenge against Amnon for raping and disgracing his sister Tamar. Two years later he had Amnon killed while he was drunk with wine. Did I mention that King David found out about the rape but did not punish his son Amnon! Well he didn't. This was truly a **dysfunctional** family. First of all, let's start with the father, David. He was the king that was upon the roof and saw another man's wife bathing herself, and he had sex with her (see II Samuel 11). Oh yes, the same David that wrote the 23rd Psalm, and said, "The Lord is my shepherd, **I shall not want".** Now that same David is secretly fantasizing and saying to himself, The Lord is my shepherd **I see what I want.** After impregnating Bathsheba, David had her husband Uriah killed on the front line of battle. This was a set-up, so that he could marry Bathsheba. During his reign as king, David had many wives. Yes, he was a polygamist!

The generational curse passed on to his son Solomon who also had an insatiable sexual desire and loved many strange women. In fact, he had 700 wives and 300 concubines (side chicks or mistresses) and they turned his heart away from God. Like father like son?

Just as David had Bathsheba's husband killed, Absalom had Amnon killed for raping Tamar. Tamar was never ever the same after her encounter with her obsessed brother from another mother!

Three Hebrew Boys

In the third chapter of the Book of Daniel, we read about three young men who found themselves between a rock and a hard place. There was a king named Nebuchadnezzar who made a golden (idol) image in Babylon. He issued a decree (law), which stated whenever the music was played, all the people were to fall down on their knees and worship this golden image. If anyone failed to bow down and worship this idol god, they would be thrown into the midst of a burning fiery furnace.

Nevertheless, there were three young men who refused to bow down and worship a man-made god. Their names were Shadrach, Meshach and Abednego. They only worshipped the true and Living God – the God that made man!

They realized that their choices had consequences, still they stood their ground. When the king heard of their refusal to bow down to his golden image, he was full of rage! He immediately had them bound and thrown into the midst of the fiery furnace, by some of the strongest men in his army. He was so angry that he commanded the furnace be turned up seven times hotter! The flames were so hot that it killed the very soldiers who threw them into the furnace!

Because of their unrelenting faith, they were "picked out to be picked on!" The three of them knew even before going into the fire, that the God they served was able to deliver. Their faith was being tested and their faith was now under fire!

Beloved, you'll never know what you're made of, until a fiery test comes your way. Sometimes in life, you have to resolve to stand up for your convictions. You have to stand for something, or you will fall for anything. I believe the three Hebrew boys made a pact before being thrown into the fire. I believe they said, "United we stand, divided we fall". They were all for one and one for all. They believed they were stronger together!

Yes, Shadrach, Meshach and Abednego were bound and then thrown into the midst of the fiery furnace. King Nebuchadnezzar thought by now, they would be burnt to a crisp. He thought he had them out of the way, that it was all over for them; you know, he thought it was a done deal. He didn't have enough sense to realize that **"It ain't over, until God says it's over!"**

When the king came close to the mouth of the furnace, he was astonished, shocked, flabbergasted, at a loss for words, because something unexpected and unexplainable happened in that fiery furnace, that he just could not figure out!

Dear Reader, there are some people in your life who are astonished, and they are still trying to figure **you** out! They don't understand or have a clue how you came through, all that you went through. You know: the cancer, miscarriages, divorce, foreclosure, losing your job and even losing a child, your breasts and your hair! They are confused, because you still have a testimony. A real true testimony means you have had a "tested life". The devil can't understand your praise. Your praise confuses the enemy. He doesn't understand how you can say you have PEACE. The truth is God may not always calm your storm, but He knows how to calm YOU down in the midst of your storm, test or fiery trial. You may not escape it, but God will empower you to bear it. Regardless of what's going on **externally,** God will empower you **internally,** so you will be able to hold up under pressure.

The astonished king Nebuchadnezzar asked this question: "Did not we cast three men bound into the midst of the fire?" He asked a question he already knew the answer to. His men replied, "Yes King". He responded by saying, "but wait a minute, I see four men **loose,** walking in the midst of the fire, and they have no hurt, and the image of the fourth is like the **Son of God**." (See Daniel 3:24-25)

Marinate on this: The king in his fury deliberately ordered the furnace to be turned up seven times hotter than it already was. What the king didn't know was that the number seven represents completion, fulfillment and perfection! Here's a word of encouragement: The Lord himself will complete, fulfill and perfect all those things which concerns you; just as he did with the three Hebrew men.

The fourth man in the fire was a Holy Ghost Fire Extinguisher by the name of JESUS. I am a living witness: when you need Him most, He will step right in on time! He will show up and show out! Is there anything too hard for the Lord? Absolutely not!

"Then the king came close to the mouth of the burning fiery furnace and said to Shadrach, Meshach and Abednego, 'You servants of the Most High God, come forth and come here!' Then they came forth and came **out** of the fiery furnace." (Daniel 3:26)

The king and his princes, governors, captains and counselors all got a close look at the three men who survived the raging fire. This fire had **absolutely no power** upon their bodies. Their hair was not singed, their clothes were not burned, and not one of them smelled like **SMOKE.** God means business when He says, "Touch **not** my anointed…and **no weapon** formed against you shall prosper" (see I Samuel 26:9 and Isaiah 54:17). We, too, must go through our own trials, tests and storms of life. They are designed to make us stronger, wiser and better.

In closing, let me say that when **you** go through, you must see yourself coming **out! Remember:** if there's a way "in it", God Almighty has a way "out of it". He has already prepared a way for your escape. If He did it for the three Hebrew men, He is more than able to move on your behalf. He will stick with you through the thick and the thin. He will stick with you until the end.

If Shadrach, Meshach and Abednego were here today, I'm certain they would lift up their voices and shout: **"We've been through the fire, but we got OUT", and we don't look like what we've been through!"**

This is a great place for a serious PRAISE BREAK!!!

10
THE FAVOR OF GOD

Favor is the Grace of God and it is a gift from God. Grace is God's unmerited favor. Favor gives us great things/blessings we really don't deserve. It also gives us what we need to accomplish the things we cannot do on our own. Favor means you have the approval of God, and He delights in your ways.

In the natural you may have limitations such as: failing to graduate high school or college; you may be up to your "eyeballs" in debt, unqualified for a loan approval; or you may be the last one to be considered for a raise or promotion.

But when the **favor of God** is upon your life, He can move people out of the way to make sure that YOU are next in line for a miracle, a break-through, promotion or loan approval. Favor does "not" mean you are perfect, for NONE of us are. But God himself will perfect those things which concern you.

You see dear Reader, when God decides to show you favor and bless you, He will cause situations to come together on your behalf, no matter what others may try to do. When you have the favor of God upon your life, the approval of others is NOT required! Favor is when the Superior and Supreme God with unlimited resources intentionally leans in your direction, in spite of your imperfections.

Please don't get this twisted. Even though the favor of God is upon your life, it does not mean you will never encounter hardships, struggles or adversities. Here are a few Biblical examples of people that had God's favor, but still encountered hardships before their victories:

NEHEMIAH. He started out as a "cup bearer" for a king named Artaxerxes. In the opening chapter of this Old Testament book, Nehemiah is discouraged because upon returning to Jerusalem, he discovered that the walls were broken down and the gates to the city were destroyed by fire. Nehemiah desperately wanted to rebuild the walls. He was a patriotic and very prayerful man. He was bold enough to request God's favor! Nevertheless, he encountered great opposition as he and the people began to rebuild the city. In the midst of distractions, he remained focused, prayerful, committed and faithful. God rewards faithfulness! Soon Nehemiah was appointed as governor. Promotion really does come from God.

After the walls and gates were restored, he closes the book (of Nehemiah) by praying, "Remember me with favor my God" (Nehemiah 13:31b). One of Satan's assignments is to keep us from asking or seeking **God's favor**. Why? The enemy doesn't want us to fulfill the purpose and calling that God has for us. Favor is crucial if we are going to have God's best for us!

ESTHER. Esther was an orphan because both of her parents died when she was young. She started out with very humble and small beginnings. The Word of God tells us NOT to despise small beginnings. This young girl was not born with a silver spoon in her mouth. She could have ended up in an orphanage, but her older cousin Mordecai took her in and raised her as his own daughter. Many people think that Esther's beauty was her greatest attribute. Not so; she was also a very humble, obedient and courageous young woman.

Esther had the favor of God upon her life, in spite of her background/history. We all have a history, but our history does not determine our destiny. Our destiny includes a pre-determined course of events that have been willed by God. Beloved, your life story has already been pre-recorded, documented and pre-determined in Heaven. Your destiny in the sight of God is just waiting to be fulfilled and to come to fruition. We tend to focus on where we are right now, what we have or don't have. BUT

GOD sees where we're going before we ever get there. He's the author and finisher of our Faith. He even knows our ending from our beginning.

When God's favor is upon our life, others will know it. But let me warn you that everyone will not embrace, congratulate or celebrate you! The "haters" won't understand how a person with your past could end up being chosen, blessed and used by God! Sweetie, "The haters are going to hate", that's what they do. Our awesome and amazing God can use the things in life that should have destroyed us and use that very thing to develop us.

Esther wound up obtaining favor in the sight of all those who looked upon her. Let me be absolutely clear about something. "What Esther started with, was not what she was **stuck** with!" Esther (the orphan) was escorted unto King Ahasuerus, into his royal palace, during the seventh year of his reign. The King loved Esther more than all the other women, and she found grace and favor in his sight. Favor isn't always fair! Because Esther remained "humble", God was getting ready to exalt her in front of all the other young virgins. The King set the royal crown upon her head and made her Queen, instead of a woman named Vashti, who was rejected by the King. God will move others out of the way to make room for His chosen ones! To God be the Glory!

Beloved, don't miss this: there may be people in your life or even in your family, who may be more experienced, better qualified, more gifted or educated than you are. But when your ways please the Lord, and He places His favor upon your life, He can elevate and promote you, in spite of. He is able to open up doors for you that no man can close. He's able to make a way out of no way. God grants you special privileges and gives you a divine "hook-up". He can even "flip the script" just for you!

Even though Esther started out as an orphan, she ended up as a Queen. The Lord God knew that her History would not change her Destiny. Esther was truly blessed to have Mordecai in her life. God also has somebody in **your** life, who can see in YOU, what you're unable to see in yourself!

JABEZ. Another person in the Bible that was favored of God was a man named Jabez. He is found in the Old Testament, in the Book of I Chronicles 4:9-10. These are only two verses of scriptures, yet they changed Jabez's life **forever.** Verse 9 says: "And Jabez was more honorable (highly regarded/respected) than his brothers: and his mother called his name Jabez, because she birthed him in sorrow". This mother evidently experienced difficult labor pains. I have met a number of women around the world, who stated they never had labor pains birthing their children.

I personally experienced labor pains for 22 and a half hours! They call it **labor** for a reason…it takes work dealing with contractions and trying to **push** the baby through the birth canal! However, once you see and hold your little bundle of joy, you feel as though the pains were all worthwhile.

Did you know that men can also be pregnant and experience labor pains? Of course, I mean they can be "supernaturally" pregnant. They can be pregnant with dreams, visions, passions, possibilities and expectations. You believe with your whole heart that you heard the voice of God saying that you would give birth to that vision **soon.** Therefore, you earnestly prayed, fasted and tried to patiently wait until you were able to give birth. But it seemed as though the waiting process was taking forever! All you wanted to do was to see your dream/vision finally come to fruition. Some of you have shared your vision with others, and they're laughing behind your back because it hasn't happened yet! Here's a word of **caution**: you can't share your vision with everybody. Why? They might not understand it, or they may let jealousy creep in and steal your vision. So please be very selective with whom you share your visions and dreams. Don't let impatience cause you to abort your expectations. They may be delayed, but not denied! Wait, I say, on the Lord's perfect timing. Be "still" and know that He is God. It's not too late to go back to school, start your own business, write a book or even produce a play.

Now let's go back to JABEZ: He asked the Lord in I Chronicles 4:10 to do the following four things: "And Jabez called on God saying, 'Oh that you would bless me indeed.'" In other words, Lord I need you to bless me in spite of my past, circumstances, limited resources, and in spite of the "labels" people try to identify me by. Reader, are YOU in need of a blessing? It's comforting to know that when God gets ready to bless you, He doesn't need the approval of anybody else! "Enlarge my coast" (my territory, my area of influence). With God, there are no limits and no boundaries. He's the God of more than enough! He's able to do exceeding abundantly above all that we ask or think, according to the power that works in us. The Bible declares that death and life are in the power of the tongue. You can open your mouth right now and speak MY GREATER IS COMING! Great doors of opportunity are getting ready to open up for me, and they will stay open, until God tells me to go through them! Don't be afraid to speak into the atmosphere, "Lord, let your hand be with me". Beloved, the hand of the Lord is strong and mighty. With His outstretched hand He wants to touch us and reassure us everything is alright, right now! He wants to touch us and restore us, strengthen, comfort and hold us. Does anybody need a touch from the Lord right now? I dare you to say, "Lay your hands on me Jesus,

I don't mind". Lord touch me one more time! "Lord, keep me from evil, that it might not grieve me". Psalm 91:10,11 says: "There shall no evil befall me, neither shall any plague come near my home. For He shall give His angels charge over me, to keep me in all my ways". Our God is a keeper. He's able to keep us from falling. Psalm 23:4 states: "Yea though I walk through the valley of the shadow of death, I will fear no **evil**: for **YOU** are with me; your rod (Your Word) and your staff (Holy Spirit) they comfort me."

If you are a Christian, you are covered in the precious Blood of Jesus, and have His DNA flowing through your veins, and NO WEAPON formed against you shall prosper. You ought to be elated that the Lord has strategically placed some people in your life who want to participate in your success and help catapult you into new heights, dimensions, depths and levels!

Lastly, When God grants you His FAVOR nothing and nobody can stop the blessings He has prepared just for YOU!!

11

GOD CAN STILL BLESS A HOT MESS

The Prodigal Son (Luke 15:11-25)

This is a very profound parable (an earthly story with a heavenly meaning). It involves a wealthy man who has two sons. The younger son requested that his father release his share of the inheritance **now,** rather than wait until the passing of his dad.

Shortly after receiving his inheritance, the younger impatient son, known as the prodigal son (a person who recklessly wastes their wealth), gathered all of his personal possessions and left home. He then traveled to a "far country" and began to live an indulgent lifestyle. I personally believe that a "far country" can be anywhere or any place where you choose to separate yourself from the will of God by doing your own thing, and by throwing caution to the wind.

Dear Reader, you can reside in a major city, or be in a room full of people, and still be in a "far country". That's a place where you find yourself literally just going through the motions, hiding behind a mask, while you try to fake it until you make it. I believe this young man was raised in a God-fearing home and had no other choice but to be in church whenever his parents went. Some of you can relate to going to Sunday School, Morning Worship and Sunday evening services. Not to mention Bible Study, mid-week service, usher and choir rehearsals. "Church, church and more church!" This young person was tired of having a curfew; he felt his parents were much too strict and enforced too many rules. He felt as though he was in prison and his parents were the guards, who enjoyed keeping him in "lock-down".

What this prodigal son failed to realize was that having godly parents can be a very rewarding yet challenging role. The two most important gifts that parents can give to their children are **roots and wings.** The Bible instructs parents to train up a child in the way he "should" go: and when he is old, he will not depart from it. (see Proverbs 22:6). Teach them the basics, such as manners, integrity, discipline, the value of a good name, the importance of education and money management. Children learn by example. They must be allowed to grow, and even make mistakes in order to learn valuable life lessons.

One day you will have to give them **wings.** You can't always be there to fix things for them. Sooner or later the apron strings must be cut, and they must leave the nest. As a loving parent, release them and allow your children to spread their wings, and trust that they will act responsibly. You keep them covered in continual prayer.

No doubt this Prodigal Son was living a lavish lifestyle. As the youth of today would say: he was partying like a rock star! He was purchasing designer shoes, clothes and jewelry. I'm sure he would have the latest iPhone, drive luxury cars, enjoy wining and dining in five-star restaurants and live in a luxurious penthouse. This young man was probably a "baller", sowing his wild oats, and was surrounded by "gold diggers". Of course, he wanted to impress his new friends, so he was undoubtedly footing the bills. But soon he found out the hard way that when you have money, your "friends" are numerous. When you're riding high, they're your best friends. But just let troubles knock at your door and they don't know you anymore. They "said" they would be with you, they "said" they had your back, and you could count on them. They "said" they were your BFF (best friend forever). But you soon found out that their forever was a very short time; and nobody wants you when you're down and out.

Luke 15:14 says, "And when he had spent **all**". (In other words this Prodigal Son was **broke, busted and disgusted!**") I can vividly imagine that his credit cards were all "maxed out"! He went to several ATM machines, inserted card after card, entered his four-digit pin, but was unable to obtain any cash, because his funds were depleted.

He was in a place and a situation that he had never been before. He was morally and financially bankrupt, due to his foolish and excessive spending. He was indeed a **HOT MESS!** In this same verse, the Bible says he began to be in want, due to a mighty famine (very little food) in that land. This young man had hit "rock bottom". He was down and out. I've learned in this journey called life, that sometimes "rock bottom" can be a good place to land, because the only way you can look, is up! That's why the psalmist David said in Psalm 121: 1-2, (KJV) "I will lift up my eyes unto the hills, from whence cometh my help. My help cometh from the Lord, which made heaven and earth".

Have YOU ever been in a desperate situation, where you realize that nobody else except God can help you or get you out of the mess you're currently in! Eventually you will realize that the ROCK at the bottom has been holding you up! Baby, that ROCK is JESUS.

Because times were so hard, this man degraded himself by taking on a menial job feeding pigs. In biblical days pigs were considered unclean animals and Jews were not allowed to touch them. For a Jewish man to stoop to feeding pigs was of itself a great humiliation, and for this Prodigal Son to desire to eat food that pigs had touched was considered deplorable!

This young man was suffering from the consequences of his actions. In life, all of our choices have consequences. However, in verse 17, he "came to himself". In other words, he had an epiphany, a light bulb or "Aha!" moment, and finally realized he didn't have to continue living this way. He was truly living beneath his privilege. This was **not** the environment he was brought up in. He said, "I will arise (I will get up, stand up and accept responsibility and accountability for my actions and move forward) and go to my father" (see Luke 15:18). In essence, "I will humble myself and admit my wrongdoings and my sins." There was absolutely no way that he could turn back the hands of time. However, he learned a valuable life lesson: be careful of the bridges you burn, because you may have to cross them again. No longer did this son want to ignore, continue in or try and cover his wrongdoings and his sins.

Romans 3:28 says, "For **all** have sinned, and come short of the glory of God". I John 1:8-10 says, "If we say that we have no sin, we deceive ourselves, and the truth is **not** in us. If we **confess** our sins, He (the Heavenly Father) is faithful and just to forgive us our sins, and to cleanse us from **all** unrighteousness. If we say that we have **not** sinned, we make him a liar, and his word is **not** in us."

However, when we acknowledge our sins, God Himself will throw all our sins into the sea of forgetfulness, to be remembered **no more.** Even though some of us were guilty of being a **hot mess**! But God dropped the charges against us, dismissed the case, and hit the "delete" button, all because of His Amazing Grace and unconditional love for us. Beloved, do you **really** understand that God loves you and me, in spite of ourselves? Right now, you need to shout, "Hallelujah!!"

Now we come to the best part of this story. Luke 15:20 says, "And he arose and returned home to his father. The son was a great distance away, his father saw him, and had compassion (love in action), and ran and fell on his neck and kissed him". No doubt this Prodigal Son was smelly, disheveled and in desperate need of a hot bath and some grooming! Yes, he was a **hot mess!** But "real" love looks **beyond all our faults** (flaws and imperfections) and sees our needs! Can I get an AMEN?

And the son said unto his father, "I have sinned against heaven, and in your sight, I'm no longer worthy to be called your son" (verse 21). This young man was truly remorseful and ashamed of his trifling behavior. He knew that he was a **hot mess**.

But thanks be unto God, this father called him by his name(son), and not by his shame (his past). I am just as excited as this Prodigal Son to find out that **God can still bless a hot mess!** The next few verses demonstrate this so lovingly!

"The Father said to his servants, 'Bring forth the best robe, and put it on him.'" The robe represents 'honor' (special recognition). "And put a ring on his hand." (The ring represents 'authority' (the power or right to give orders/make decisions). "And put shoes/sandals on his feet" (see verse 22). The sandals represent 'freedom'. In those days, slaves were not allowed to wear sandals. Sandals were reserved for a free man. Hallelujah, whom the son sets free is free indeed!

This Prodigal Son was blessed to have a Father who never stopped caring, loving or praying for his son to come to his senses. This Father patiently waited for his son to get back on the right track. He did a P.U.S.H. (Prayed until something happened). Dear Reader, prayer still works!

In verse 23 we read that the father said, "And bring the fatted calf, kill it and let us eat, and be merry". In other words, "Fire up the grills, we're going to have a great celebration!"

In verse 24 the father declared, "For this my son was dead" (spiritually). (Please note that he did **not** disown his son!) "But now he is alive again; he was lost and is found. And they began to be merry and celebrate". Do you want to know the real reason they were celebrating?

In Luke 15:7 it says, "There will be joy in Heaven over ONE sinner that repents (turns away from sinful behavior). When we repent, we're telling the devil that we are getting back in our rightful position and returning to the God who made us.

Some of us have lost homes, possessions, friends, family members, and almost lost our minds! But instead of having a nervous "breakdown", God came in the nick of time, and gave us an awesome "breakthrough!" I don't know about you, but I'm so glad that my God is still in the blessing business. In spite of ourselves God is still loving, keeping, protecting, forgiving and healing us.

What I'm about to say is **not fake news:** God is the God of another chance, and **He can still bless a Hot Mess!**

The Woman at the Well (John 4:1-38)

In the fourth chapter of John, is a story about Jesus and a Samaritan woman who met at Jacob's Well. This well was known as a meeting place for women who conversed with one another while drawing water. Samaritans intermingled and inter-married with foreigners and also adopted their idolatrous ways and were therefore considered "half-breeds". They were despised and rejected by the Jewish community.

Jesus was weary because He been traveling from city to city teaching, preaching and healing. At the noon day hour, He sat down on Jacob's Well. I think it's absolutely amazing that Jesus (a well of water, was sitting on a well of water)! The Samaritan woman now enters the picture, and a dialogue begins.

This woman came to draw water, and Jesus said unto her, "Give me a drink of water". Shocked at His request, this ostracized woman said unto Jesus, "How is it that you being a Jew, asks of me (a Samaritan woman) to give you a drink (see John 4::9)" In other words, "You know that you Jews do not associate with Samaritans".

This meeting was no chance encounter. It was the beginning of a brand-new life for her. This appointment was her date with destiny!

Jesus responded by saying in verse 10, "If you only knew the gift of God, and who it is who says to you 'Give **me** a drink,' you would have asked Him, and He would have given **you** living water".

Jesus was up to something concerning this woman, and He already knew that she would **not** leave His presence the same way that she came! No, she would never ever be the same again!!

In verse 11, we read "The woman said to Jesus, 'Sir you have nothing to draw with and the water is **deep** (*75-100 feet deep*), so tell me where you can get this living water?'"

In verses 13-14 (NIV), we see His response: "Jesus answered, 'Everyone who drinks this water will be thirsty again, but whoever drinks the water that **I give,** will **never** thirst, because the water that I give will be like a well of water springing up into eternal life.'"

In the 15th verse, this woman mistakenly believed if she received this water that Jesus offered, she would not have to return to the well each and every day. She did not immediately understand what Jesus was talking about. Sometimes we have to ponder and "marinate" on what's being said before we can absorb it all in. Most of the time we tend to be resistant to change because we are creatures of habit. It takes time to accept something that challenges and changes the very foundation of our lives!

Jesus told her, "Go get your husband and the two of you come back". In the 17 and 18th verses, the woman answered and said, "I have no husband". Jesus replied, "You are correct when you say you have no husband".

The fact is you have had **five husbands**, and the one you're with now, is **not** your husband".

Jesus is OMNISCIENT (He knows ALL things). He read her life like an open book! You see, when we get "real" with God, He will get "real" with us! He loved her in spite of her imperfect life!

By this time, the woman realized that Jesus was a true Prophet and that He was the God of another chance. Indeed, He was a God of restoration and Amazing Grace!!

She was so excited that she left her water pot. In other words, she left her old way of living and embraced her brand-new life.

II Corinthians 5:17 says, "Therefore if any man or woman be in Christ, he or she is a new creature: old things are passed away; behold **all** things are become new". This changed and brand-new woman went into the city and said, "Come, see a man who told me all the things that I ever did. Could this be the Christ?" OMG, only God can turn our **mess into our message.** Because of her testimony, others went out of the city and came unto Jesus and received salvation and deliverance.

This story ought to let every "religious demon" know that

your history, does not determine your destiny! God, with His good self can turn a promiscuous woman into an **evangelist!!**

It would be very remiss of me not to give my personal "spin" to this story. This Woman at the Well was guilty of looking for love in all the wrong places and faces. She felt she had to have a man to complete her. She couldn't bear the thought of being alone. Let the records show that a man can spot a desperate and vulnerable woman from a mile away! Sometimes women can be college-educated but clueless when it comes to a man. Often times our better judgement escapes us, and we tend to **settle** for a man that would not work in a pie factory. We **settle** for a man who has no ambition, integrity, who shows us little or no respect, who expects us to take care of them, who has multiple sexual partners, and treats us simply as a "booty call". Yes, I said that! Precious sisters, you can do bad by yourself! There is a saying that goes like this: "A piece of man is better than no man at all!"

The devil **is** a liar. Beloved, we teach people how to treat us. So, you have to love and respect yourself before others love and respect you. Stop settling! Stop lowering your standards! There is a "queen in you", so wait for your "king!" Meanwhile, you must learn to love, accept and embrace the "skin that you're in".

Stop waiting on a mother's son to validate you. Be confident in who the Creator created **you** to be. You are not meant to be a clone or a carbon copy of any other woman. Although you may feel like your life is in shambles and broken pieces. Remember this: God can take broken pieces and turn them into masterpieces.

Don't you dare be so desperate for a man that you de-value yourself by allowing a man to demean, disregard, disrespect or dishonor you. You are unique, worthy, powerful and priceless. Don't let anyone else on earth tell you what you're worth. Take this moment in time and look in the mirror, and repeat, "Lord, open my eyes and help me believe that I am what **you** see!" You are fearfully and wonderfully made.

Be careful of what or whom you seek after. Remember, the Woman at the Well was seeking for things that could not satisfy her. But one day she had a close encounter with JESUS, who extended the opportunity for her to draw from a well that never ever runs dry.

If you are in need of a divine intervention and visitation from above, I challenge YOU to call on the name of JESUS. He's waiting to hear from YOU!

12
GOD IS UP TO SOMETHING CONCERNING YOU

Philippians 1:6 says: "Being confident of this very thing, that HE that has begun a good work in **you** will perform it until the day of Jesus Christ". Psalm 138:8a says, "The Lord will perfect that which concerns me". When it looks like things in your life may never get any better, or when it seems like all hope is gone, and **you've** done all that **you** know to do, let the records show that there are some things in your little life that nobody can do for you, but **God.** When you can't see your way out, God has already prepared a way for your escape!

When you're down to nothing, just remember that God is up to something concerning **you!** I want to encourage you by saying: Don't you dare give up or throw in the towel! We've all made our share of mistakes, gotten off track, missed the mark, blown it. Perhaps you have stumbled and fallen, but Beloved, you don't have to be perfect to be loved by a perfect God!

God is Up to Something Concerning YOU

I Peter 5:7 says, "Cast **all your care** upon the Lord, because HE cares for **you**". Others may not give you the time of day, but God is genuinely concerned about you. He knows the plans that He has for you. In fact, God knows all about you. He knows about your history, your baggage, your faults and flaws, as well as your imperfections and short-comings. Nevertheless, God still chooses to move on your behalf. When the pressures of life are weighing you down and it seems as though your world is falling apart, it could actually be falling into place. The very things that you perceive to be **blocking** you could very well be God's way of **blessing** you. His ways and thoughts are so much higher than ours! You must believe that your Heavenly Father knows best, even though you may be clueless why He allows certain things to happen. He's moving in ways you don't understand right now. In the meanwhile, you just **be still** and know that He is God all by himself! He is able to open up doors that have been closed in your face. He is able to calm your storms and give you peace that passes your understanding. He's able to make a way out of no way, and to prepare a table for you in the **presence** of your enemies. God is able to give you **favor**, even after a **failure!**

Marinate on this: If God can change **coal** into **diamonds, sand** into **pearls,** and **caterpillars** into beautiful **butterflies,** He is certainly able to change things in your life.

Romans 8:28 declares. "And we know that **all things** work together for good to them that love God, to those who are the called according to **His purpose**". It may not "feel good" while we're going through the process, but ultimately, it's working **for** our good! What God has for YOU, it is for YOU! God really does care about you, and He's behind the scenes working **all things out for YOU.** So Precious One, do what God says to do in **Proverbs 3:5- 6.** "Trust in the Lord with **all** your heart; and don't lean to your own understanding. In **all** your ways acknowledge **Him,** and **He** will direct your paths".

God created you, therefore He knows all about you. He knows your ending from your beginning, the number of hairs upon your head, He even knows your thoughts before you think them. He has plans to intentionally bless you in spite of your trials. God is up to Something concerning YOU! You have His guarantee that HE will finish what He started. He will complete what He has begun, and HE will do just what He said!

If you are a child of the True and Living God, I **dare** you to repeat these words, while laying hands on yourself! "He that has begun a work in ME, is faithful to perform it." I have **greatness in me, potential and possibilities. I really do believe that MY GOD is up to something concerning ME!"**

My Real Testimony

In order to have a "real testimony", you must first have a "tested life". Life won't always be sugar, spice and everything nice. Sometimes life can throw you a curve ball that totally rocks and wrecks your life! But God can use everything you've gone through to make you who He's called you to be!

As I reflect over the course of events in my personal life, I can vividly recall performing my first eulogy at the precocious age of nine. My father was a sergeant in the Army, and was stationed in Etain, France.

I had a beloved ladybug named "Lady" and eventually she passed. I was so heart-broken and devastated. I asked my mother if I could have a funeral for Lady in our back yard. She smiled, gave me a big hug and consented. I also pleaded with my mother to allow me to wear her black hat with the veil; after all, I was in mourning. I appointed one of my girlfriends to sing Amazing Grace, and one of my male classmates to be the deacon and lead us in prayer. They both graciously consented. Little did I know that as a little child, God was preparing me for a divine calling! Jeremiah 1:5a states: "Before I formed you in the belly, I knew you; and before you came forth out of the womb, I sanctified you".

I loved Lady so very much and was convinced in my heart that she loved me too! I could barely contain myself, looking at my Lady lying motionless in that mason jar. After performing Lady's committal, I told my friends that it was time to CRY. My female classmate replied, "I'm not crying over a stupid ladybug!" OMG, I let my nine-year-old raw emotions get the best of me, smacked her and said, "I bet you're gonna cry now!" Of course, she ran and told my mother, who insisted that I apologize for hitting my friend. I did and with tears still in her eyes, she forgave me for laying "unauthorized hands" on her. With a sincere heart, I also asked JESUS to forgive me and He did. Isn't it wonderful how the Lord will show us mercy, even when we mess up? That's truly Amazing Grace in action! I have been preaching the Glorious Gospel of Jesus Christ for over 30 years now. I am proud to let the world know that I am not perfect yet; but I serve a Perfect God who is "perfecting" all of my imperfections.

Dear Reader, my life has been full of tests, trials and storms. My testimony is real! I am a survivor of molestation, rape, domestic violence, racism, armed robbery, bullying, depression, low self-esteem, car wrecks, multiple concussions, gangrene in my leg, and ovarian cancer! Praise the Lord: I don't look like, what I've been through!!

I know how it feels to have people try to judge and label you because you don't fit into their "cookie cutter" image. It took me some years, but I have been delivered from what other people say about me. If the truth were to be told, many of those who are trying to judge and figure me out, are secretly trying to emulate me. But they really don't have a clue of what I've had to endure, nor do they realize the high cost that I've had to pay because of the anointing upon my life! I preached a message a couple of years ago entitled, "The Anointing attracts Attacks". Nevertheless, I can now Dare to be Different and, more importantly, Dare to be ME.

Just like YOU, I have a past, but my past has been forgiven, deleted and blotted out. I am so happy that the LORD did not erase my future because of my past! He saw the BEST in me when others could only see the WORST in me. Many said that I would never make it, BUT GOD brought me through and GOD brought me OUT.

I can now boldly declare that every generational curse attached to my life has been cancelled. Every chain has been broken, every stronghold has been pulled down, every shackle has fallen off. My burdens have been removed, my joy has been restored, and every yoke has been destroyed! My head is lifted up above my enemies all around me. I confess that I am walking in my liberty, because JESUS has set me free, and whom the Son sets free, is free indeed. I am more than a conqueror, because my **history** does not determine my **destiny,** and my **condition** is not my **conclusion.** I am elated to know that what I **started** with, is NOT what I'm **stuck** with. That's my story and I'm sticking to it!

I believe what the Word of God says in I Corinthians 2:9, "But it is written, EYE has not seen, EAR has not heard, neither has it entered into the HEART of man, the things which God has prepared for them that love Him". I am who I am today, because God used everything I went through to help make me the woman I am today. I can't take any of the credit, by the Amazing Grace of God, I am what I am!

Because I am still here, I truly believe that the **rest** of my days shall be the **best** of my days. I am **believing** GOD for open doors of opportunities, supernatural favor, increase, a greater level of anointing, with the wisdom to know how to handle it. I am ready to receive an overflow of blessings, pressed down, shaken together and running over. So, don't count me out because this is MY SEASON! Lastly, Revelation 12:11 states, "And we overcame him (Satan, the deceiver) by the blood of the Lamb (JESUS CHRIST) and by the word of **our testimony.**

As I look back over my life, I can truly say that I've been blessed, and I am a **living testimony.**

I Know for Myself that God Can Turn It Around

Romans 8:28 declares: "And we **know** that **all things** work together for good to them that love God, to them who are the **called** according to **His Purpose**". I know for myself that God is still able to turn things around. I'm not talking about what I heard through the grape vine or read on Twitter. I am a living testimony of the awesome power of God and how HE alone can flip the script and change things in our lives.

I know that God can open doors that were once closed in my face. I know that He can pick me up, turn me around and place my feet on solid ground. I know that God is a way-maker. He can make a way out of no way; because according to John 14:6, Jesus said, "**I am the Way**".

I know that the Lord is able to deliver on time, for He has delivered **me** out of **all** of my troubles. I know that He is a healer too, for Exodus 15:26b (KJV) says, "I am **Jehovah-Rapha**, the Lord that healeth thee." Psalm 103:3b (KJV) says, "HE healeth **all** my diseases. Isaiah 53:5b states: "And with HIS stripes we are healed". Somebody other than me ought to be glad that **every sickness is not unto death!**

I know that MY God can lift up a hung down head, just as the scriptures say in Psalm 24, verses 7-10. Dear Reader, I also know that the Lord can turn my weeping into joy. I'm so glad that weeping may endure for a night, but JOY comes in the morning! I know for myself that God can give you the garments of praise for the spirit of heaviness (see Isaiah 61:3). Somebody who feels **weak** right now, needs to be reminded that His strength is made perfect in your weakness! Yes beloved: The **joy of the Lord is your strength.** If you allow Satan to steal your joy, he can snatch your strength! You need to tell the devil he is a liar, because **this joy** that you have: the world didn't give it, and you refuse to let the world take it away!

Have you ever had your back up against the wall, and it seemed as though there was no light at the end of the tunnel? Have you ever felt as though you were falling apart at the seams, and were close to having a melt-down or a nervous breakdown? But just in the nick of time, God with His "good self" stepped right into your situation, and instead of a **break-down**, God came in with a mighty **break-through**? I don't know about you, but right about now, I feel like **shouting**, because He turned my **dilemma** into my **deliverance! Hallelujah!!**

I know when my enemies (and my frenemies) were all around me digging ditches, plotting, scheming, speaking against me falsely and desiring to see me fall and fail; the

Lord delivered me from the hands of my enemies! Won't He do it? I absolutely love this scripture in Psalm 23:5a, "HE prepares a table before me in the **presence of my enemies"**. In other words, God wants your enemies to see that HE has blessed you, favored you, promoted, elevated and anointed you in spite of them! Those enemies are ticked off because they thought if they didn't like or support you, or include you in their circle, that you would surely fall and fail. **"BUT GOD!"**

Right about now, you should feel like sending your enemies a "Thank You" card. Because of them, and in spite of them, God intentionally moved on your behalf! He showed up and He showed out, and you know without a doubt, that **all the Glory** belongs to God!

I know when the storms of life are raging, that the Lord is able to keep you in **perfect peace,** because HE is the Prince of Peace and that means He's able to give you a peace that passes all understanding.

I know that God is still in the Blessing Business, and when HE says, "I WILL BLESS YOU", He just does it because He can. It doesn't matter about your **vocation, location, education or your devastation!** Regardless of where you grew up, how dysfunctional your family tree may be; in spite of your "jacked-up" credit, your past, or who is in the White House; REMEMBER that God is still on the

THRONE. His amazing power supersedes everything else!

In closing, I want to let the devil know that MY GOD is GREATER, STRONGER and MORE POWERFUL than anything or anybody in the whole world!

ABOUT THE AUTHOR

Nancy F. Lowery was born in Hempstead, New York, and has been a long-time resident of North Carolina. She has been married to her husband Malcom for 41 years. They have one daughter, Shana, who resides in Virginia. All three are proud veterans and have traveled extensively.

Nancy studied at Southeastern Community College in Whiteville, North Carolina, and Cameron University in Lawton, Oklahoma.

Her mantra in life is: "As long as I have a **pulse**, I have a **purpose**." She is an ordained elder and apostle, a prayer warrior, intercessor, liturgical dancer/instructor and a **spiritual** body builder. Nancy has been preaching and teaching the Gospel of Jesus Christ for 32 years. She founded and pastored the Pillar of Truth Christian Ministries in Kannapolis, North Carolina for 10 years. She is the former owner of Chosen Vessels Cleaning Services.

About the Author

Nancy operates in the Ministry of Helps by building up pastors and leaders who have become discouraged and "battle weary" from the pressures of leadership.

Nancy is the author of an inspirational book entitled: **"Are YOU a Chosen Vessel?"** This is her second book, and she gives **all** of the credit, glory and honor to her personal Lord and Savior, Jesus Christ.

www.ingramcontent.com/pod-product-compliance
Lightning Source LLC
Chambersburg PA
CBHW071720040426
42446CB00011B/2145